MacLehose Trail Hong K

Murray MacLehose, the territory's longest

term of office, from 1971 to 1982, coincide

of Hong Kong from a laissez-faire entrepot

competitive financial centre, and the cautious opening up of China.

Within a few years of the tall Scotsman's arrival in the colony, flotillas of
Vietnamese boat people converged on this crowded territory, adding to
its population pressures. Hundreds of thousands of refugees from Mao's
Cultural Revolution already lived in hillside squatter huts. MacLehose
presided over the establishment of the Housing Authority, and the
founding of new towns to accommodate the burgeoning population.
The Cross-Harbour Tunnel was opened, linking Hong Kong Island to
Kowloon. The first MTR line came into service. MacLehose had an
unprecedented meeting with Deng Xiaoping, and broached the matter
of the New Territories' expiring lease for the first time.

But perhaps his greatest achievement was the establishment of the
Independent Commission Against Corruption, an autonomous body tasked
with rooting out rampant bribery in public life. The Hong Kong police, until
then known as 'the best force money could buy', was a tough nut to crack.
Mass arrests were made, and policemen fled overseas. Three thousand
officers demonstrated against the new measures and even attacked the
ICAC headquarters, but the culture of corruption had been smashed.

Democracy was introduced to local councils, but MacLehose resisted
direct elections to the legislature for fear of inviting Chinese rivalries
onto Hong Kong soil. "If the Communists won, that would be the end
of Hong Kong," he said. "If the Nationalists won, that would bring in
the Communists."

The MacLehose Trail follows interlocking ridges from east to west to
take in most of the high peaks of the New Territories. It is at its busiest
during the annual Trailwalker event, when thousands of hikers join forces
to complete the 100km distance for charity.

MacLehose Trail

The first long-distance trail to be laid out, and still the best known, the MacLehose owes its popularity at least partly to the annual Trailwalker event. But it has its own unique charms. As well as scaling Tai Mo Shan, Hong Kong's highest peak, the trail follows a

good proportion of our most attractive coastline. The magnificent string of beaches at Tai Long Wan appears on many must-do lists, and it's not just hikers returning: turtles were recently found nesting here for the first time in decades.

Stage	Route
Stage **1** **Pak Tam Chung 北潭涌**	Pak Tam Chung 北潭涌 > Long Ke 浪茄
Stage **2** **Long Ke 浪茄**	Long Ke 浪茄 > Pak Tam Au 北潭凹
Stage **3** **Pak Tam Au 北潭凹**	Pak Tam Au 北潭凹 > Kei Ling Ha 企嶺下
Stage **4** **Kei Ling Ha 企嶺下**	Kei Ling Ha 企嶺下 > Tate's Cairn 大老山
Stage **5** **Tate's Cairn 大老山**	Tate's Cairn 大老山 > Tai Po Road 大埔公路
Stage **6** **Tai Po Road 大埔公路**	Tai Po Road 大埔公路 > Shing Mun 城門
Stage **7** **Shing Mun 城門**	Shing Mun 城門 > Lead Mine Pass 鉛鑛坳
Stage **8** **Lead Mine Pass 鉛鑛坳**	Lead Mine Pass 鉛鑛坳 > Route Twisk 荃錦公路
Stage **9** **Route Twisk 荃錦公路**	Route Twisk 荃錦公路 > Tin Fu Tsai 田夫仔
Stage **10** **Tin Fu Tsai 田夫仔**	Tin Fu Tsai 田夫仔 > Tuen Mun 屯門

Distance in km	Duration	Challenge
10.6	3.00	*Easy rambling*
13.5	5.00	*A fairly challenging walk*
10.2	4.00	Strenuous hiking
12.7	5.00	Strenuous hiking
10.6	3.00	*A fairly challenging walk*
4.6	1.50	*Easy rambling*
6.2	2.50	*A fairly challenging walk*
9.7	4.00	*A fairly challenging walk*
6.3	2.50	*Easy rambling*
15.6	5.00	*Easy rambling*

total **100**

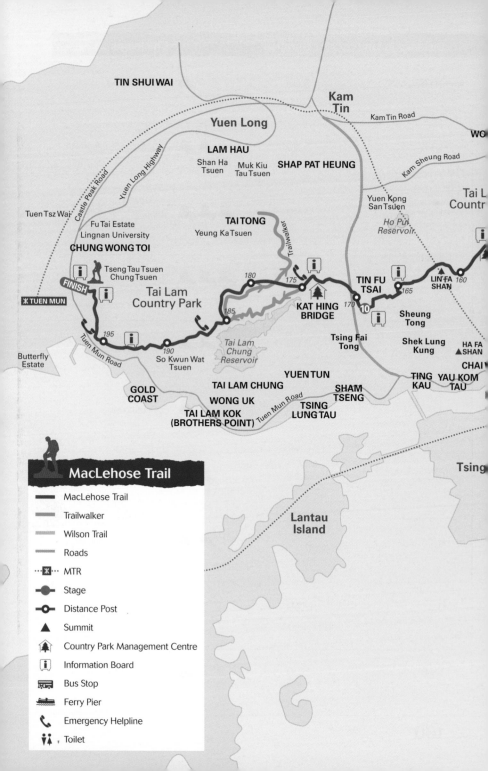

The Visitor Centre has an exhibition hall which is well worth a look, as it gives you a better understanding of the country you are about to cover. This location is also the launch point for the annual Trailwalker race: thousands of participants crowd behind the barrier, waiting to be let loose on the 100 km trek.

Teams line up for the start of the annual Trailwalker race

Take the road straight ahead beside a wide rocky riverbed, passing on your right a small bridge which leads to Sheung Yiu, a restored fortified village now run as a folk museum. Continue along the road, passing on your left the Pak Tam Chung Village sign. At the road junction, pass the turning to Wong Shek Pier on your left and continue straight ahead. At the corner, among a cluster of signposts you will find a mapboard indicating the start of the MacLehose Trail. However, the first of the following 200 half-kilometre markers makes its appearance on the right-hand side of the road a little further on, just as the trail starts to rise. The road makes a steep ascent between two hills until it reaches a point overlooking the vast High Island Reservoir.

The great wall holds in place a mighty weight of water

M006 Zigzag tack to the water sports centres

Hong Kong has always been short of water, and imaginative schemes have been required to address the problem. This reservoir was created by joining an offshore island to the mainland by way of three dams. The vast enclosure thus formed was then filled with fresh water. In English, both the former isle and the reservoir are named High Island, but not so in Chinese, which identifies the island as Leung Shuen Wan, or Provisions Boat Bay, and the body of water as Man Yee, or Many Possibilities. Thus when you turn right at this second junction, you step onto Sai Kung Man Yee Road.

It was only during the construction of the reservoir that roads were built as far out as Pak Tam Chung and Wong Shek. Prior to this, the road was much shorter, stopping near Tai Mong Tsai, and the Sai Kung peninsula was far less accessible. This waterworks road is officially closed to traffic, including cyclists, but you will see (and hear) a growing number of green taxis making their speedy journeys out to Long Ke, whether legally or otherwise. On weekends, sinewy joggers pant back and forth along the road, probably in preparation for the Hong Kong Marathon.

High Island Reservoir – solution to water shortages

The first of the two major dams is crossed, allowing views of the watersports centre and parts of the coast of Rocky Harbour (previous spread). Further on, a viewing compass below Tai She Teng (Big Snake Peak) points out places of interest between the trees. The MacLehose Trail sticks rigidly to the road, but a semi-circular detour may be made from here, at some length, to the bays on the rugged southern coast: Pak A and Tung A villages at *M012*, with their respective seaside temple and seafood restaurants, and Pak Lap at *M015* with its abandoned village and Gurkha-built pier, are each worth a visit. At *M018*, a monument to perished construction workers heralds the final dam. Giant concrete dolosses, one of which is placed in commemoration on the waterfront in Sai Kung town, stand against the force of the open seas. Cross the dam and turn left at its far end. Near the rest pavilion at *M019*, toilet facilities are available. From here head in the direction of Long Ke, climbing a rugged stone trail to the north.

This section of the trail ends at a strange choice of locations, on the hillside overlooking Long Ke. To regain public transport, either retrace your steps to Pak Tam Chung or do what most hikers opt for, follow Stage 2 as far as Chui Tung Au.

M018 Mighty dolosse, a memorial to one of many

M018 Mighty dolosses hold back the Pacific Ocean

M019 Bulwark against the approaching tide of the South China Sea

The reservoir [is] a trapped sea channel

MacLehose Trail

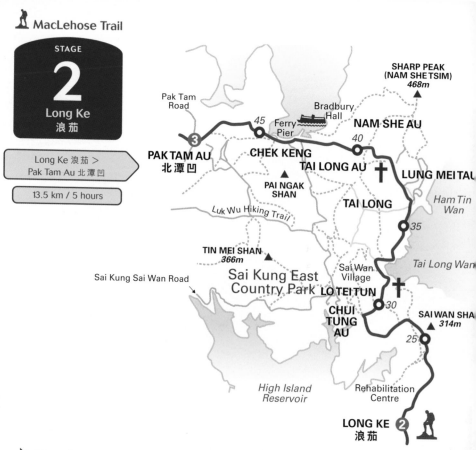

STAGE
2
Long Ke
浪茄

Long Ke 浪茄 >
Pak Tam Au 北潭凹

13.5 km / 5 hours

Pak Tam Road

SHARP PEAK
(NAM SHE TSIM)
468m

Bradbury Hall

Ferry Pier

45

NAM SHE AU

40

PAK TAM AU
北潭凹

CHEK KENG

TAI LONG AU

LUNG MEI TAI

PAI NGAK SHAN

TAI LONG

Ham Tin Wan

35

Luk Wu Hiking Trail

TIN MEI SHAN
366m

Sai Kung East
Country Park

Sai Wan Village

Tai Long Wan

Sai Kung Sai Wan Road

LO TEI TUN

30

SAI WAN SHA

CHUI TUNG AU

SAI WAN SHA
314m

25

High Island
Reservoir

Rehabilitation
Centre

LONG KE
浪茄

2

Starting at Long Ke

Most hikers walk Stage 2 as a continuation of the preceding section, or join it some way along at Chui Tung Au. This latter point, at the end of Sai Wan Road, may be reached by taking a minibus or green taxi (tel: 2729-1199), from Sai Kung town, and then walking a short stretch along the northern edge of the reservoir.

Rural rehab in lush surrounds

While descending to Long Ke from the south, the aquatic emerald colours of the bay below (following spread) may distract you from preoccupation with your aching knees, resulting from countless stone steps and cement paths. An old fishing boat lies abandoned on the shore. Heralded by *M021*, the beach is a sample of what lies ahead at Tai Long Wan; fine sands, breaking rollers and a huddle of small houses in the wide, flat valley behind. The settlement

Beached and bleached

in this case however is not a victual-dispensing village store but a Christian-run drug rehabilitation centre, with surely the best setting of any in Hong Kong. Along a path of soft sea sand, a short distance ahead you will come across a fresh water tap. Replenish supplies here, as there are no sources of water on the trail before you reach Sai Wan at *M030*.

Step on it: open views but no shade

M020 *The aquatic emerald colours of Long Ke Bay*

Out on a limb: deeply indented coastline

M026 *The mapboard of Sharp Peak and Tai Long Wan*

The path continues up the ridge on the other side, easily visible as there is little tree cover. Shade is provided only by two newly erected pavilions, the first of which is perched on the ridge at *M023*, almost halfway to Pak Tam Au. From here, for the next 400 metres, it's an arduous climb up a flight of uninspiring and foot-crunching concrete steps. Some time later, the peak of Sai Wan Shan is achieved, where a second pavilion provides shelter at *M025*, with spectacular vistas of Sharp Peak and Tai Long Wan as your reward for making the arduous climb.

Winding downhill, the path reaches a crossroads at Chui Tung Au (Blowpipe Pass). The beach and fir trees of Sai Wan beckon temptingly far below. If you need to finish your hike here, turn left to aim for the end of Sai Wan Road, where a taxi (tel: 2729-1199) may be called or a rare minibus may be waiting. For Sai Wan, turn right to descend by way of more cement cast stairs.

Sai Wan glimpsed from afar

Weekend aspiration; the two deserted beaches of Sai Wan

Sai Kung is unusual in that its villages possess more churches than temples. This is due to the strenuous evangelical zeal of missionaries like Father Volonteri, an Italian priest who tramped this peninsula in the 1860s, long before these parts of the New Territories were leased to Britain. Many villagers converted to Catholicism. While the liturgy was conducted in Latin, the European priests often learnt Hakka to communicate with the local people.

As you walk beside the wide creek to enter Sai Wan, its small ruined church can be seen in undergrowth to your right. The idyllic village makes a living these days from providing refreshment to passing hikers; three or four cafés are open, selling the usual range of coffee, beer, fried rice and noodles. One of the elderly restaurateurs has a broad Mancunian accent as a result of

working in northern England as a youth, formerly a common practice among New Territories villagers. No sign of an economic downturn here. Business is brisk and the village, especially on weekends, offers a choice of seaview restaurants with expanded menus and supplements its income by renting beach paraphernalia.

There are two beaches, both with lovely stretches of sand. The trail leads through the village to cross a bridge and heads north over the rocks and then through tall grasses which back the wide beach, bounded by a tidal rivulet. Pools lie upstream. At the far end, you're obliged to turn inland to cross the bridge – unless the tide is out, in which case you have direct access to the mounting coastal path.

A rugged coastline confronts the Pacific Ocean

You must now clamber over a substantial headland. The coast below is pounded by the waves of the Pacific, creating the welcome sting of salt water in the air. At the top at *M035*, the twin beaches of Ham Tin Wan and Tai Wan are spread at your feet, the appropriately named Sharp Peak standing over them like a watchful guardian (following page). This is apparently where Lord MacLehose himself would take sanctuary, ferried out by helicopter for a private swim, when matters of state weighed too heavy.

At the bottom of a long flight of stairs, the trail hits the gorgeous sands and then immediately veers left, leaving the coast behind to proceed over soggy swampland; instead, you may wish to cross the beach, where a pair of makeshift restaurants sit on the far side of a wide creek. Tents, surf and boogie boards are available for rent, along with an ample supply of cold drinks and fast food. And more conspicuously so at weekends. A precarious bridge of wooden planks spans the water, somehow bearing the combined weight of hikers bound for these cafés. You may follow the path through Ham Tin (Salty Fields) village, over a cowpat-strewn helipad, to join the MacLehose once more further upstream.

M033 Weekend respite in Sai Wan's sheltered waters

From *M033*, until the trail meets the main road at Pak Tam Au beside *M049*, one might as well be walking in the urban jungle. The way ahead for the next 8 km has been sanitized by a pathway of bare concrete, with no effort made to incorporate local stones or rocks into the cement. It's an unimaginative 'rural improvement', as these works are termed (following page). Even the local cattle have left their expressions of disapproval upon this urban intrusion.

M036 Shaded weekend respite

The next village is Tai Long, where a couple of shops open at weekends to cater to parched and hungry walkers. Besides the standard fried rice and noodles, plum soup and home-made herbal tea are also available. Part-time surfers keep their boards in the otherwise empty and ruined houses. Some lad has carried a KMB bus stop sign over hill and dale, 5 km from the nearest road, to place it in his front yard. Don't wait for a bus here.

Sai Wan and Tai Long Wan: jewels in Hong Kong's natural crown

Take care to turn left at the well-preserved church at the head of the path. You now face a reasonably difficult climb to the top of the pass, with great views of the open bay behind you. Coming down the other side, the two arms of Long Harbour end in thick greenery below.

Refreshments ahead – but only on weekends

The path meets the pebbly coast near the ancient but empty village of Chek Keng. At *M043* a toilet of *avant garde* design has made its recent appearance. You can make an exit from the trail here by turning right and walking along to the pier, which is served several times a day by the Tolo Harbour ferry. Or you can hire (but negotiate the fare in advance) a

M035 Deceptively calm, beach and breakers beckon on sunny days

M033-M049 Government speak, 'beautification' and 'improvement'

speedboat at a charge of roughly $30 per head, depending on how many are in your group, for a quick and exhilarating sprint over to Wong Shek, where bus 94, from Sai Kung terminates or departs, whichever way you look at it. A very hospitable youth hostel sits on the hill above the pier, handy if you are engaged on a longer trek. Mr Wong has been running the place single-handedly for the past 12 years.

M043 Ferry arrival at the Youth Hostel

Chek Keng has a church and many houses, most of which are still standing amongst the fallow fields; it must have been a busy town in its day. It may become busy again, if the

M044 Long Harbour

construction of a substantial pier is any sign. On exiting the village through the trees, continue along the right hand path. The trail carries on westwards, slowly climbing a hillside. At *M045*, bear left uphill in the direction of Pak Tam Au — and not straight ahead downhill in the direction of Wong Shek Pier, as one might be inclined to. Another detour is possible just further on, along a somewhat overgrown path which leads to the enchanting hamlet of To Kwa Peng — which seems to be inhabited by just one old lady — and thence to Wong Shek.

The MacLehose continues up a gradual incline to reach Pak Tam Au, the end of this long section. Here you'll find a recently erected 5-star toilet facility which has won both acclaim for its view, and criticism for spoiling it!

Bus 94 from the near side of the road runs back to Sai Kung town, joined by the 96R Diamond Hill bus on Sundays and holidays.

MacLehose Trail

3

Pak Tam Au
北潭凹

Pak Tam Au 北潭凹 >
Kei Ling Ha 企嶺下

10.2 km / 4 hours

> ## Starting at Pak Tam Au

From Sai Kung Terminus, take bus 94 or 96R on Sunday and public holidays in the direction of Wong Shek Pier. Alight a few stops short of the terminus, at Pak Tam Au, the highest point on the Pak Tam Road. It may be best to let the driver know your destination. Alternatively a taxi ride from Sai Kung Town costs roughly $70.

YUNG
SHUE O

CHEUNG
SHEUNG

NGAM TAU SHAN
▲ 452m

55

50

3

PAK TAM AU
北潭凹

WA MEI SHAN
391m

NGAU YEE SHEK
SHAN

60

65

KAI KUNG SHAN
399m

LUI TA SHEK
379m

LUNG
HANG

Kei Ling Ha
Lo Wai

Sai Kung West
Country Park

PAK TAM

KEI LING HA
企嶺下

WONG
CHUK
YEUNG

70

4

Sai Sha Road

WONG MO YING

TAI MONG TSAI

Lady MacLehose
Holiday Village

Rolling uplands

M045 *Another busy day at Pak Tam Au*

Sheltered woodlands near Sai Sha Road

Facing the road, the trail begins 50 yards to your left, on the opposite side adjacent to the bus stop. On the near side is a tiny village hidden in the greenery. The hike wastes no time in mounting the hill ahead up an impressive stone staircase. From *M049* onwards it's back to hiking as it should be – over pebbles, earth, fallen leaves and roots – and you're tempted to take long strides from boulder to boulder. Spare a thought for the country parks team that manoeuvred these boulders into place, some weighing tonnes. Marker *M050* makes its appearance on your left. Tree cover soon graduates into grassland (following page). The ascent of Ngau Yee Shek Shan (Cow's Ear Rock Mountain) gives wonderful views of the rolling country covered on Stage 2.

A more level section leads to Cheung Sheung, a high, hidden plateau crossed by a bewildering mix of paths. Here a solitary stone bench awaits occupation. Wild cattle try their best to obstruct the way onwards. At *M055*, cross the bridge overshadowed by a venerable tree, to the Hui Lam Store, a small lean-to café in its own cluster of trees, serving home-made dau fu fa (sweet beancurd dessert) and soya milk, hot or cold. The ancient proprietor opens shop on weekends only. Returning to the trail, you will find that straight ahead lies Jacob's Ladder, a precipitous descent to Shui Long Wo. We however bear left at *M055* and turn left again at the next fork to head south, skirting the flanks of Wa Mei Shan and then, after passing through a cool valley filled with birdsong, approach the next peak of Lui Ta Shek (Thunderstruck Rock). The path keeps to the western side from *M058*, and hikers are refreshed by cool breezes blowing from Tolo Harbour. An escape route is possible to Pak Tam Road soon after *M059*, a sprint of 2.7 km or about I mile.

Down in the valley, you are sheltered by walls of trees and brush on either side. Ignore the turning for Shek Hang at *M062*, for yet another ascent is on today's schedule. The climb up Kai Kung Shan (Rooster Mountain), until you reach *M064*, is demanding, partly tree covered over a severely eroded clay track caused by monsoon rains rushing unchecked down both sides of the hill, but its 399-metre summit affords a 360-degree panorama over striking ranges of hills in all directions. The island-strewn waters of Port Shelter to the south are balanced by the simple coastlines of Tolo Harbour to the north. Directly below, Three Fathoms Cove is edged by stands of mangroves. To the west looms the dark shape of Ma On Shan, boasting almost twice the elevation of the hill you've just climbed — and the next stage passes close by its summit.

It's rather exposed between *M062* and *M065*, and the welcome breezes can become forceful crosswinds in bad weather. After a level ridge walk, the path descends gently through woodland, over trails strewn with aromatic pine needles down a long slope of stone steps shaded by trees to Sai Sha Road. There you will find picnic spots with ample tables and deluxe toilet facilities on both sides of the road. Buses 99 and 299X travel back to Sai Kung town, or you could cross over and catch the 299X going in the other direction to Sha Tin.

Chicken run: the stretch towards Rooster Mountain

Running cool to the muffled murmur of a creek

M050 Timeless trail: the MacLehose leads on

Ma On Shan is still-yet distant, beyond the mists of Tolo Harbour

MacLehose Trail

STAGE 4

Kei Ling Ha 企嶺下

Kei Ling Ha 企嶺下 >
Tate's Cairn 大老山

12.7 km / 5 hours

MA ON SHAN

Ma On Shan Tsuen

Disused Mine

WONG CHUK YEUNG

KEI LING H 企嶺下

75

LUK CHAU AU

Lutheran Grace Youth Camp

80

PYRAMID HILL (TAI KAM CHUNG) 536m

70

SHEK LUNG TSAI

MUI TSZ LAM

NGONG PING

NUI PO AU

Mau Ping Village

85

Ma On Shan Country Park

UK CHEUNG

WEST BUFFALO HILL 604m

FU YUNG PIT 514m

TSIM MEI FUNG 393m

90

BUFFALO PASS (TA SHE YAU AU)

TATE'S CAIRN 大老山 95

Gilwell Scout Campsite

TATE'S CAIRN (TAI LO SHAN) 577m

TUNG YEUNG SHAN

> ## Starting at Kei Ling Ha

Take the MTR to Sha Tin and board the 299X from the bus station beneath New Town Plaza. Alight just beyond Kei Ling Ha Lo Wai, at a point where a side road branches off for Yung Shue O. You can also get here by taking the 99 or 299X from Sai Kung.

Camping on the trail at Shui Long Wo

The trail commences on the western side of Sai Sha Road, heading initially south from *M069* but soon turning left to join a quiet service road, which rises uphill. At this point untreated but fresh stream water is available on tap. A note of caution; be assured of an ample supply of drinking water before heading on, as there is no reliable source of water en route until you

M074 Stepping skywards on stony staircase

reach the dependable stream at *M094*. Pass the Shui Long Wo campsite on your right, and then make a left turn onto Chuk Yeung Road to carry on past the radar station, also situated on your right.

The MacLehose turns left off the tarmac road onto a dirt track at *M073*, just before the deserted upland village of Wong Chuk Yeung (Yellow Bamboo Ocean), and then swings into dense forest with lush young bamboo groves on either side, turning right at *M074* to join a flight of steps pointing skyward. Although steep, if taken cautiously, the ascent offers perfect climbing conditions under cover of shade. Once high ground has been achieved, views of Sha Tin and Sai Kung open up below. Ma On Shan (Horse Saddle Mountain (following page), named for its distinctive shape) is still an intimidating prospect ahead.

The path continues up a trail of packed clay and rocks, this time with little shade cover but blessed with refreshing gusts of wind, and then ascends sharply to a point below the summit of the mountain at *M078*. A steep climb indeed, as Ma On Shan is the second highest peak in the New Territories at 702 metres — and you must make a detour (well recommended) if you wish to enjoy the helicopter-style views from the top. Then the trail strikes south along a well-defined ridge towards evenly shaped Pyramid Hill. You can choose to cross it or follow the MacLehose around its base.

Serious trails for serious hikers: The saddle ridge of Ma On Shan

M076 Saddle up: approaching Ma On Shan

The high plateau of Ngong Ping enjoys wide open views of Port Shelter and its family of islands. An escape route leads down to Po Lo Che, near Sai Kung. Down to the west, an old iron mine once employed 2,000 miners, but was closed in 1976 – just a few years before the country park was established.

Carrying on across Delta Pass, where there is little trace of the former Mau Ping villages marked on the map, we walk between the peaks of Fu Yung Pit (Farewell Hibiscus) and Buffalo Hill, where lush groves of young bamboo bow to the prevailing winds as they line both sides of the path, to descend gradually across the southern side of West Buffalo Hill. The stone steps are taxing on old knees but the trail soon levels out to continue in the shade of trees. Wide valleys below, thick with forest and largely inaccessible to man, are filled with the songs of unseen birds. Beside a covered shelter beneath age-old trees, a signpost points downhill to Gilwell Camp, 7 km ahead.

M093 Every path has its puddle

From the covered shelter at *M082* until you reach *M085*, it's again perfect hiking with quite unusual views over the multitude of bays and inlets that constitute Sai Kung.

Further ups and downs deliver the hiker to a narrow road beside the Gilwell Scout Campsite, near *M093*, which shares its name with a similar camp in England. If you're not a woggle-wearing member of the Scouts, permission to camp at the site is required in advance – call the Scouts Association of Hong Kong on 2957-6488. However, should you arrive without the required piece of paper, the site attendant has authority to grant permission, according to the signpost. The minor peak behind the site is notable not for its Chinese name, Tung Yeung Shan or East Ocean Mountain, but for its hopeful-sounding English appellation, One Rise More, which has disappeared from the maps. After completing this cosy stretch some elevation between *M085-M089* is inevitable, but in compensation you enjoy pleasant hiking conditions under tree cover. Here dedicated Country Parks personnel have laboriously laid an impressive stretch of boulder pathway from *M088-M089* but inexplicably it abruptly ceases and one is deposited back on a clay path.

The trail heads through thick forest over rocks and offers steady progress on an even plane from *M089-M093*. A short distance further it takes a sharp right and arrives at the first dependable source of flowing fresh water since we advised you to bottle-up at *M069*. Here too is a table with benches idyllically located, providing a welcome spot for a much needed snack break.

It's all downhill from here

Losing track: the trail descends into forest

Knife-edge trail over Pyramid Hill

At *M094* the trail reaches a service road. Turn right and head downhill for a short distance. It then bears abruptly left into the undergrowth. At *M098* it exits onto Fei Ngo Shan Road, overlooking an exceptionally wide panorama that spans Lei Yue Mun Channel to Central District. A rest pavilion and toilet facilities are provided here.

M085 The natural harbour at Hebe Haven

Stage 4 ends at this point. To reach public transport, you could turn left and follow Fei Ngo Shan Road down to the Clearwater Bay Road. It's a long way however, and you are probably better off following Stage 5 as far as Sha Tin Pass and descending to Wong Tai Sin from there.

The hills around Kowloon have witnessed the city's evolution

MacLehose Trail

STAGE

5

Tate's Cairn
大老山

Tate's Cairn 大老山 >
Tai Po Road 大埔公路

10.6 km / 3 hours

> ### Starting at Tate's Cairn

This section begins just beyond Gilwell Camp. Short of hiking the previous stage, the only way to reach this spot is by foot or taxi up steep Fei Ngo Shan Road. The best place to catch a cab is from Choi Hung MTR station: take Exit A3, up the escalator and through the shopping mall.

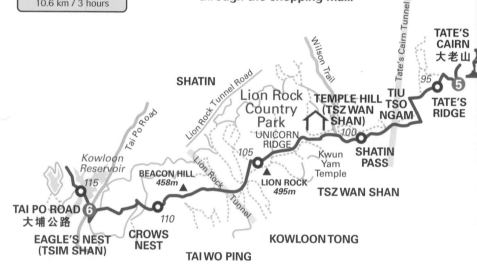

Valleys of birdsong stretch away from Kowloon

M101 Emerald-hued shrine under Temple Hill

Follow the road until it forks, with Mau Tso Ngam village nestled in the valley below. Turn left onto the trail, entering a damp-leaf forest filled with the sounds of running water. The path eventually turns directly uphill over grass to Tate's Ridge, passing remains of wartime emplacements before coming down to join Jat's Incline, a road built by military engineers. Jat is an Indian name.

This great vantage point over Kowloon (following spread), accessible by car, has been used in countless Hong Kong movies. Turn right to follow the mountain road along the ridge, going straight ahead at the junction under Temple Hill (Gentle Cloud Mountain). Down the slope lies the attractive green-roofed Kwun Yam Temple, dedicated to the Buddhist goddess of mercy.

At Sha Tin Pass there is a café serving noodles and cold drinks. Pictures of celebrities who have visited the café plaster the walls inside, a great resource if you have ever wanted to see a photo of Chow Yun-fat eating fried eggs. This point marks the halfway stage of the MacLehose Trail, with marker *M101*, and is also crossed by the Wilson Trail. Walk downhill to the first hairpin bend and regain the forest path at the entrance to the Lion Rock Country Park, clearly marked by a wooden archway. A flight of steps leads in short order

M050 Low-rise Kowloon Tong, now free of airport height restrictions: a realtor's dream come true

Lion Rock ageless symbol of Kowloon's Dragon Hills with Tai Wai in the background

Block capital: industrious East Kowloon

to an easy ridge path thankfully under tree cover, and marker *M102* soon makes its appearance. Spectacular views of Kowloon and Hong Kong Island are glimpsed between the trees. A mere 100 metres north and we find ourselves again in lush green countryside with no trace of the urban sprawl. From here until *M108* one is hiking again in perfect conditions on clay paths in the close proximity of trees, rustling branches and birdsong. This ridge was part of the Gin Drinker's Line, a system of defensive fortifications meant to keep

Behind enemy lines: Lindsay Ride escaped internment

invaders at bay, and you will see occasional remnants of this in the form of ruins, and distance markers, all the way to Shing Mun. At *M104* is an intersection with a path heading up to Lion Rock Peak. At *M106* there is an interesting comment by the son of Lt Col Lindsay Ride, who having read his father's diaries, recalls that when his father escaped wartime internment and checked the defences, he observed that these same concrete markers inconveniently revealed the location of the defences to the enemy. From *M103* to *M115*, one is again hiking under ideal conditions uncontaminated by concrete paths.

M106 Defence locations revealed to the enemy

Amah Rock can be seen to the north, overlooking Sha Tin. We pass a side path leading up to the airy double summit of Lion Rock. Then, just past the wooden shelter erected on the right by Friends of Mountain Wayfarer, a rambling group, we reach Kowloon Pass, with its recently-built pavilion and clear view down to Kowloon.

From here the path leads along a gentle contour in the direction of Beacon Hill, with impressive views of Lion Rock and the winding MacLehose Trail behind, and the handsome Kowloon Peak standing further off to the right. KCR trains bound for China rumble somewhere far beneath your feet as they travel by tunnel under the Kowloon range.

Cast in Rock – the Amah still waits

At *M108*, a short climb amidst young bamboo offers amiable hiking on earth and stone steps and brings you out onto a Civil Aviation Department service road at *M109*. Cross it and mount the steps past the radar dome, which crowns Beacon Hill. In dynastic times

Below Lion Rock: Kowloon stretches to the harbour's edge

Ancient path, as well-established as the forest

gone by, fires were lit on the hill to give warning of invaders. Now, it serves to direct air traffic. To the north, one can see in succession the higher peaks, which we will be traversing later. From this narrow path at *M110*, provided overhead branches and the haze don't obstruct the view, one is offered panoramas of West Kowloon with its elegant Stonecutters Bridge.

M109 Beacon Hill

Descend Beacon Hill by way of the path which crosses the Lung Yan service road several more times. "Beware green bamboo snake!" reads a scrawled message in Chinese. Beside the rain shelter at *M111*, the MacLehose turns right to skirt the northern side of Eagle's Nest, home to kites rather than eagles. However you can turn left to circle the southern side, giving yourself the opportunity to see the evening lights coming on in Kowloon. The sodium-lit container terminals at Kwai Chung appear more attractive at night than they do by day.

Verdant Unicorn Ridge

Autumn aspect: a soft carpet of leaves

Either route ends at a country parks service road, which runs downhill a short way to the main Tai Po Road at *M115*. If the greenery is not too far overgrown at *M113*, you'll catch glimpses of the 1910-vintage reservoir with its precision-curved granite walls holding back tons of water in the monsoon season (following spread). Macaques swing through the trees and hang around hoping for scraps. Feeding these insistent monkeys is supposedly prohibited, but you will see pet-adoring locals who have brought carrier bags of food to feed them. Turn right down the surface road to exit via the Eagle's Nest Nature Trail archway. If the Tai Po highway at this point is too congested to cross, turn left and traverse by way of the footbridge 100 metres further on. Bus 81 will carry you to the MTR at Prince Edward.

MacLehose Trail

STAGE

6

Tai Po Road
大埔公路

Tai Po Road 大埔公路 >
Shing Mun 城門

4.6 km / 1.5 hours

Jubilee Reservoir

SHING MUN
城門

7 125

Shing Mun Tunnel

Wilson Trail

Smugglers' Ridge

Lower Shing Mun Reservoir

120

GOLDEN HILL

Wilson Trail

Kam Shan Country Park

Shek Lei Pui Reservoir

Kowloon Reservoir

TAI PO ROAD
大埔公路

6 115

> ## Starting at Tai Po Road
> Take the MTR to Sham Shui Po
> station and leave by Exit D2. Walk
> straight ahead up Kweilin Street
> to Tai Po Road. Aim uphill, passing
> the Garden Biscuit Factory on
> your left, to find the bus stop
> opposite the North Kowloon
> Magistracy. Buses 72 or 81 will
> take you up to Piper's Hill and
> the start of Stage 6. Alight as the
> bus crests the rise, where the
> footbridge crosses the road and
> macaques are awaiting their daily
> food deliveries.

Macaque eyes alert in all directions

M115 *The Kowloon reservoirs are replenished by the streams of Tai Mo Shan*

Water catchments at Kam Shan Country Park are home to mountain monkeys

Still as a stone, a native amphibian

The trail starts just ahead, at *M115* located on your right, where Golden Hill Road branches off to the left. This is the entrance to the Kam Shan Country Park, a small but well wooded park which surrounds the four reservoirs of the Kowloon hills.

Pass between the Kowloon and Kowloon Byewash Reservoirs. The Golden Hill Road from *M115*

M115 Pristine waters of the Kowloon Reservoir

leads gently uphill alongside picnic sites and barbecue areas until *M121*. This is a busy section of the trail, frequented by noisy herds of barbecue aficionados. At the Kam Shan Family Walk intersection the two governors' trails briefly meet again under the darting eyes of dozens of macaques, who at times outnumber the picnickers. The crowds thin out a little before a fork is reached, at which point we turn left, passing a plaque commemorating the inauguration of a section of the Wilson Trail. The route then leaves the tarmac to head into the countryside along a path parallel to Smugglers' Ridge.

At *M121*, alongside a wooden pavilion and mapboard, the path bears right in the direction of Shing Mun Reservoir. Here you're thankfully off the hot service road and back into natural terrain, though not entirely as the

Seven dragonfly species are native to Hong Kong

concrete tends to intrude from time to time. You're now approaching the ruins of the Shing Mun Redoubt, centrepiece of a warren of defences designed to hold the Kowloon hills against attack from the north. This complex of tunnels, pillboxes and lookout posts, manned by the Royal Scots, saw intense fighting in the first stages of the Japanese invasion. Its fall on the 9th December 1941 prompted the evacuation of the entire Kowloon peninsula, and the retreat of the defending forces to Hong Kong Island.

Today the remains are in reasonably good condition and can be explored. Tunnels leading into the complex are marked 'Regent Street,' 'Shaftesbury Avenue,' 'Strand Palace Hotel' and so on; London place names which would have given a measure of assurance to troops stationed half a world away from

M123 Tunnel vision: abandoned trenches

home. Japanese names are also carved into the tunnel walls. Bring a torch if you wish to follow the tunnels any distance; certain sections have collapsed and it is easy to lose yourself in the maze of trenches.

From the high points of this ridge, you're able to survey Tsuen Wan and Tsing Yi to the west, and the giant massif of Tai Mo Shan to the north. Following the MacLehose downhill leads you to a busy barbecue site bordering the Jubilee Reservoir. Turn left to walk along the tarmac road to Pineapple Dam, which recalls the fruits grown by the former Hakka villagers of the area. Before the reservoir was created, this place was known as Pineapple Pass. At the end of the monsoon season it's reassuring to see

Oxford St – a measure of assurance for troops stationed half a world away

the reservoir brim full, if not overflowing, as Hong Kong can then remain largely reliant on its own supply of water.

Minibuses 82 and, on Sundays, 94S run from the visitor centre down into Tsuen Wan, where you can pick up the MTR. Or you can walk down Shing Mun Road, the lower section of which is lined by scrap-filled junkyards, to the bus terminus at Lei Muk Shue.

MacLehose Trail

STAGE
7
Shing Mun
城門

Shing Mun 城門 >
Lead Mine Pass 鉛鑛坳

6.2 km / 2.5 hours

Shing Mun Country Park

TA TIT YAN

Wilson Trail

LEAD MINE PASS
鉛鑛坳

GRASSY HILL
647m

135

SHEK LAU TUNG

AU PUI WAN

WONG CHUK YEUNG

130

Yau Oi Tsuen

*Jubilee
(Shing Mun)
Reservoir*

Wilson Trail

NEEDLE HILL
532m

125

SHING MUN
城門

❯ Starting at Shing Mun

Take the MTR to Tsuen Wan, leave the station by Exit B and follow the walkway across to Shiu Wo Street. Board green minibus 82 for Shing Mun. At Pineapple Dam, turn right to walk along the edges of the Jubilee Reservoir, busy at weekends, to the start of Stage 7 at a barbecue site.

Weekend chefs galore

The MacLehose crosses the larger main dam in tandem with the Wilson Trail, offering views of far-off Lion Rock and of the rocky stream, which later becomes the Shing Mun River Channel. At the end of the crossing it parts company with the Wilson Trail, bears briefly right and then left up a service road to be greeted by the Stage Seven wooden archway and mounts a spur of Needle Hill. Starting at

Scouting out new horizons

Reservoir spillway and the foothills of Tai Mo Shan

Brimful, the reservoir after heavy summer rains

Flash flood: The rushing waters of a mountain stream

M125, for the next kilometre it gains altitude up steep stone steps. After a stretch of sandy path it descends and climbs again on cement steps.

The steps are steep but have the benefit of delivering you to vantage points fairly quickly. The Jubilee Reservoir below was completed in 1937, deriving its name from the silver jubilee celebrations of King George V, and was the largest of its day. It catches the waters of countless streams flowing down the wooded slopes of Tai Mo Shan and Grassy Hill. In fact the ridgeline borders of Shing Mun Country Park follow almost exactly the watersheds of the hills surrounding the reservoir.

Shing Mun means Walled City Gate, a reference to a former fort erected in this commanding area in the 17th century. The Ming general who chose the location evidently thought along similar lines to the British, who built their Shing Mun Redoubt in the same vicinity 300 years later.

Stone staircase up Needle Hill

M127 Sha Tin with Lion Rock on the horizon

The long, winding and predominantly stone staircase is interspersed with stretches of clay track as it mounts two lesser peaks before reaching the tip of Needle Hill. The path is paved on both incline and decline with tedious concrete steps, though in the lower regions many have been washed away by torrential rains. Moving northwards along the ridge, you walk a high route between placid waters and green hills to the west, and the packed valley of Sha Tin to the east. From this viewpoint you can imagine Sha Tin as it was before the new town: a wide, sandy estuary dotted with traditional villages, fields green with young rice. Some of the villages still remain, squeezed in between the high-rises, but acres of reclamation have banished Tide Cove to a name on old maps.

The trail joins a service road near *M129*, which carries on across open grassland. Overhead, jumbo jets prepare for their final descents into Chek Lap Kok. If you turn your ear to the wind, you can almost hear the flight attendants' instructions to fasten seatbelts, stow tables and return headsets. Welcome tree cover overshadows the road in the vicinity of *M131*. On the right one passes a wooden arch announcing the way to Shatin Town, which offers an escape route should you wish not to continue. Turn right at *M132*

Jubilee Reservoir: a feat of 1930s engineering in the lee of Tai Mo Shan.

to begin the ascent of Grassy Hill. A little higher up, a left turn gives the option of an easier route to Lead Mine Pass if you don't feel up to the climb. It descends gently on a partially shaded service road.

On the way up to the summit, the hiker enjoys unobstructed views of Needle Hill and other peaks to the south. Then, from the top, the wooded lands to the northeast, forming part of the Tai Po Kau special area, extend to the shores of Tolo Harbour.

Descend by way of well-built stone steps to Lead Mine Pass. Turn left, and then right, as you meet the road. The Wilson Trail crosses the MacLehose here for the last time. A picnic site is furnished with a new pavilion, swish toilet facilities, tables and benches, and two sets of mapboards. To return to Shing Mun, follow the paved track downhill, keeping to the western edge of the reservoir when you reach it. To finish at Tai Po, and get home by MTR, take the trail which leads downhill to the north, commencing behind the toilet block, and catch minibus 23K to the MTR station. Both escape routes are of roughly equal length.

M128 A dragon's back ridge above Tai Po Kau

MacLehose Trail

STAGE
8
Lead Mine Pass
鉛礦坳

> Lead Mine Pass 鉛礦坳 >
> Route Twisk 荃錦公路

9.7 km / 4 hours

The watering hole at Lead Mine Pass

> ## Starting at Lead Mine Pass
This section of the trail is lengthened by the necessary walk to its starting point. Lead Mine Pass can be reached from Pineapple Dam by taking the waterworks road steadily uphill from behind the Country Parks Visitor Centre; or from Tai Po Market MTR by taking green minibus 23K past Wun Yiu to San Uk Ka, and walking uphill; or from Tai Po Kau nature reserve by taking bus 72 from Lai Chi Kok MTR station as far as Tsung Tsai Yuen, and then following the woodland track as it winds its way around the northern side of Grassy Hill. All routes entail lengthy approaches to Lead Mine Pass.

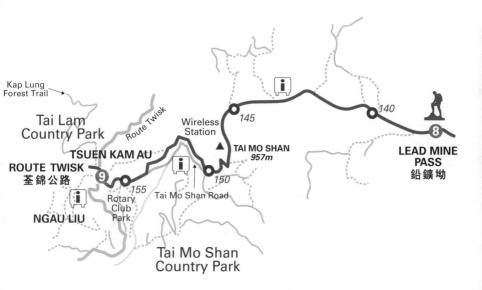

M147 Approaching the very summit

The clearing at the pass contains the usual collection of country parks facilities in the shape of mapboards, toilets and picnic areas. Metals other than lead were once mined in the area, tungsten among them. Enter through the wooden archway marked MacLehose Trail Stage 8. Our way leads initially up a steep flight of steps — many of the treads coming from the wooden rail sleepers used in the mine's tunnels — and soon joins a boulder-strewn ridge path. It's great hiking, twisting along narrow sandy trails, and it grows pleasantly cool as you approach the upper ridges of the pass. The lights of the beacon ahead shine through the high-altitude mists.

Tai Mo Shan (Big Hat Mountain) is the highest peak in Hong Kong at an elevation of 957m. Look for the faint traces of stone ribs, which line the sides of the mountain and nearby ridges. Their origin is unclear but they are thought to be the remains of ancient tea terraces. Certainly wild tea from the slopes of Tai Mo Shan was picked by local villagers until modern times.

M140 Tea break: cutting through the tea terraces

Gentler aspects of Tai Mo Shan

Keep to the ridge path as it doggedly mounts the eastern spur of the mountain. This cloud-gathering peak is well known for its inclement weather, but if conditions allow, fabulous views of the eastern half of Hong Kong are available on your ascent. Just after *M143*, a fork with a mapboard is reached. For the next five kilometres from here until you reach *M152* it's a downhill plod on tarmac. The right-hand path leads sharply downhill to the Lam Tsuen valley, passing the wonderful Ng Tung Chai waterfalls along the way. Now our course lies ahead on a narrow and somewhat weather-beaten paved road, resulting from the contrasts in weather conditions these high reaches endure, for the last stretch to the summit.

You pass a disused military installation on your right, fenced and shuttered since British forces departed. The sign warns 'Government Property — Unauthorized Entry Prohibited'. Who holds the key to the lock and sliding bolt, both now rusted solid? Then, a little higher up through windswept scrubland, the radar station occupying the summit comes into view. The gates to the compound are wide open, but you can't go in — two lethargic dogs raise a low growl to warn wanderers off, their ferocity somewhat lessened by the litter of energetic pups dancing around them. *M147* on your left sits on the highest point in Hong Kong.

Over the top and down again

Coming down the other side, the road negotiates a series of hairpin bends as well as frequent all-enveloping clouds of mist. The rocky, wind-battered landscape recalls hikes in far cooler climates. To circumvent the meandering hairpin bends, hikers have voted with their boots and created shortcuts dissecting the route. *M152* heralds a lonely road junction formerly guarded by a Gurkha sentry box. The left turn leads along a contour to the Sze Lok Yuen youth hostel. Here, On 1 October 2009, the Agriculture, Fisheries and Conservation Department implemented a route change from this point on until the trail meets Route Twisk. This was probably decided upon to avoid Sunday drivers and big-headed bikers in colourful crash helmets who hog the narrow track at considerable speed, in danger of colliding with week-end hikers.

On your left, a few metres downhill a MacLehose sign indicates a flight of slate steps descending into the greenery. From here until you reach *M156* you're on the newly designated country path route.

M152 Route change from this point on

The trail crosses the main road and at *M153* encounters a pleasant picnic area with rain shelter pavilion. It then ascends briefly on stone steps weaving its way through boulders, under partial tree cover (following page). Away from the busy road it's very much back to nature with the sounds of bird song and the occasional cow patty punctuating the dirt track ahead. Here the route is justly popular for its spectacular panorama of Kam Tin and the western New Territories. The airfield runway at Shek Kong and the Mai Po wetlands beyond Yuen Long both reflect the afternoon sunshine.

At *M156* the trail reaches the visitors centre with toilet facilities for 'Ladies and Gentlemen', provided you arrive between operating hours 9:30 am-4:30 pm. Well-located signs point the way ahead. As the trail meets the road, passing on your right the grave site of what must have been a very prominent member of the local community, judging by the enormity of the tomb and its feng shui designated

M153 Unmistakably — the way ahead

location, follow the sign pointing up steps to the bus stop on the near side of the road from where one can more easily traverse Route Twisk ('Tsuen Wan Into Shek Kong').

Three's company

Bypassing busy Tai Mo Shan highway

At this point the trail emerges to mark the end of Stage 8. From the bus stop on the near side of the road, take bus 51, bound for Nina Tower, down to Tsuen Wan MTR. I once boarded this bus in the early evening to find it completely occupied by a party of high-spirited Nepalese, who were singing, clapping and dancing in the aisles. If you have a similar journey, do sample the vegetable samosas, but try not to miss your stop at the flyover above the MTR station.

Free range cattle

Sign of things to come

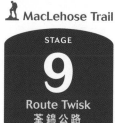

MacLehose Trail

STAGE
9
Route Twisk
荃錦公路

Route Twisk 荃錦公路 >
Tin Fu Tsai 田夫仔

6.3 km / 2.5 hours

> ## Starting at Route Twisk

Take the MTR to Tsuen Wan, leave by Exit A and turn immediately left to mount the steps to Tai Ho Road. Catch bus 51 to Tsuen Kam Au, getting off at the head of the pass near the sign reading 'Welcome to Yuen Long.' Alternatively, a taxi to this point costs about $50. The trail leads off the main road to the left, past the Country Parks Management Centre at *M156*. Cross the barrier to join the concrete service road.

Ho Pui Reservoir

Tai Lam Country Park

LIN FA SHAN

ROUTE TWISK
荃錦公路

160

165

170

TIN FU TSAI
田夫仔

PAK SHEK KIU

SHEUNG TONG

TSING FAI TONG

M153 Grand theft auto: Do you recognize your vehicle, Sir?

Various minor trails branch off the leafy path. Tai Lam Country Park is the second-largest of all, stretching westwards from Route Twisk to Tuen Mun. Although its name refers to a kind of Chinese olive tree, the area was seriously deforested and eroded until post-war years. Its current green character is due to afforestation to protect the catchments of Tai Lam Chung Reservoir built in 1957.

This part of the trail is also a bicycle route. For the next 20 kilometres until you reach *M197*, you're hiking on a mix of concrete or tarmac surfaced service roads. Follow the road which bears right in the direction of Tin Fu Tsai. It's easy sun-stippled walking, with occasional views of the Pat Heung (Eight Villages) plains to the north. At the crest of the first incline at *M157*, bear left. On the right is a helicopter-landing pad. At *M159* benches are provided from which to view Tsuen Wan, with its controversial Nina Wang Skyscraper Tower, the three Lantau-Link bridges and also the elegant Stonecutters Bridge. From *M160* it's downhill for a stretch. Ignore the road turning to the left, which

Counterfeit commandos in action

leads to Lin Fa Shan, a site of disused tungsten mines. At *M165*, intersecting with a picnic area and covered pavilion, the path makes a turn to descend south, and later on at *M170* you stumble upon a fenced-off war games arena, a motley collection of burnt-out car carcasses and empty fuel barrels strategically placed to represent tanks and bunkers. In the hills above you may come across Sunday soldiers, accountants and import/export clerks in full combat gear, stalking each other with knock-off Kalashnikovs. Spare a

M174 *After a sudden downpour – waters in motion*

thought for the real soldiers of the PLA who are stationed all across Hong Kong but are confined to barracks. The trail continues its gentle descent until it reaches a three-way intersection at the confluence of a river, just under a bridge. Continue on along the right hand track.

The end of this section at Tin Fu Tsai is reached shortly afterwards. A picnic site is watched from above by wild macaques, eyes peeled for scraps.

As with Stage 2, it's an odd place to finish, convenient only if you are

Pendulous petals in bloom

camping and can make use of the campsite nearby. Otherwise, continue on to Stage 10, or carry on a short while until the Yuen Tsuen Ancient Trail departs to the left. This joins a paved track which takes a convoluted two-hour descent to Tsing Lung Tau on Castle Peak Road. Buses from the near side of this road run back to Tsuen Wan.

Captivated by the rush of cascading water

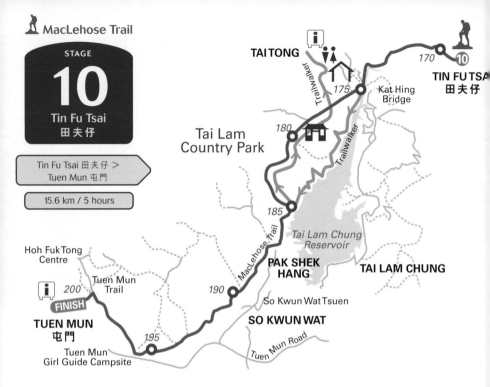

MacLehose Trail

STAGE

10
Tin Fu Tsai
田夫仔

Tin Fu Tsai 田夫仔 >
Tuen Mun 屯門

15.6 km / 5 hours

TAI TONG

170

**TIN FU TSAI
田夫仔**

10

Trailwalker

175

Kat Hing
Bridge

180

Tai Lam
Country Park

Trailwalker

185

Tai Lam Chung
Reservoir

TAI LAM CHUNG

Hoh Fuk Tong
Centre

200

Tuen Mun
Trail

MacLehose Trail

190

**PAK SHEK
HANG**

So Kwun Wat Tsuen

FINISH

**TUEN MUN
屯門**

195

Tuen Mun
Girl Guide Campsite

SO KWUN WAT

Tuen Mun Road

› Starting at Tin Fu Tsai

This section is best tackled as a continuation of the shorter Stage 9, since joining its start from elsewhere involves a walk almost as long as Stage 9 itself. It can however be reached by taking green minibus 96M from Tsuen Wan MTR station to its terminus at Tsing Lung Tau, and then following a maze of tracks uphill past Yuen Tun and Tsing Fai Tong. Bring your map.

Passing through the valley of Tin Fu Tsai, the MacLehose keeps to the paved road to reach the Wing Kat (Forever Lucky) Bridge at the picnic spot adjacent to an old gnarled tree, and then to the 19th century Kat Hing Bridge, where the MacLehose makes its second directional change. At this point the route is redirected uphill on the service road from its former route along the shoreline of the Tai Lam Chung Reservoir.

Hikers debate

The sea refuses no river

We now no longer turn left to walk beside the brook but follow instead the cement service road uphill. The relocated Marker *M175* soon appears on your right. From here it's a challenging incline with occasional rest stops. Thick, lush forests line both sides of the way up. At the intersection at *M177*, the trail bears left on a continuation of the service road while the Oxfam Trailwalker heads right in the direction of Tai Tong. Signs stridently proclaim that mountain bikers are no longer permitted along this stretch of the MacLehose Trail.

Long-limbed strides downhill

At the cul-de-sac with the MacLehose marker and the Trailwalker OTW191 signs, mount the stone steps in the direction of Wong Nai Tun Reservoir. At this point we find ourselves walking in the opposite direction to the Trailwalkers. From here on it's again very pleasant hiking on sand track, avoiding boulders, crossing tree roots and stepping widely over rushing streams, especially during the monsoon season. At *M179*, an abandoned Chinese style house cum altar occupies the intersection. A trail marker points down to the shoreline of the reservoir.

M179 Abandoned homestead, crossroads landmark

M184 Topped-up reservoir after seasonal rains

M184 *Panorama of lush vegetation encroaching on the reservoir*

Lush foliage short of the urban area

At *M183*, the trail again joins a service road. Follow it downhill, enjoying on your left exceptional views of the lush vegetation encroaching on the multi-curved shores of the reservoir with mainland China in the distance.

At *M186* spare a moment to admire the superb masonry of the one-kilometre-long Pak Shek Hang granite dam wall. It's admirable to see how stonemasons of yore worked with such precision and dedication.

At *M187* the Trail takes a sharp right uphill to reach the Tai Lam Chung Water Catchment. From here on for the next six kilometres it's level walking, as if taking into account the fact that any strenuous hiking would be less than welcome considering the number of markers one has already traversed from Pak Tam Chung near Sai Kung.

The eroded spurs of Kau Keng Shan (Nine Paths Mountain) rise on your right as you look down over the Gold Coast and across to Lantau. Some enlightened slope stabilization work has been done along here, with vegetation already growing through the bio-degradable netting. Small-scale agriculture is still carried on in places beside the trail, tanned villagers carrying water to their plots in bamboo-balanced buckets.

Water-bound blossoms

As the path turns north, the vast new town of Tuen Mun fills the view ahead. The authorities have done a splendid job of constructing picnic sites, viewing pavilions and fitness stations with chin-the-bar, parallel bars, tendon stretching, push-ups, and jump-and-stretch challenges — probably intended for local residents rather than hikers, who will have little energy left after completing the previous 98 kilometres. With the setting sun the striking profile of Castle Peak (following spread) stands watch over the far side of the bay. This sheltered anchorage, close to the approaches to Canton, was used by pioneering Portuguese explorers as far back as the early 1500s.

Tilling the land

Prince Charming under leaf cover

M190 The last of the catchment curves

M198 Castle Peak bathed in twilight

At the end of the catchment, as the trail, together with the fading daylight, peters out, take the stone path on your left, passing under the wooden archway. The trail finally descends, by way of newly laid stone steps lined on both sides with canary-yellow bomb-proof railings, and past untidy squatter huts and a reeking nullah, to the Castle Peak Road at its junction with Pui To Road: a name which recalls a monk with supernatural powers who lived on the foothills of Castle Peak over a thousand years ago. Despite its historical allusions, it's a very modern, urban end to a trail which has led the rambler through such magnificent natural scenery.

Reaching a settlement: At trail's end, the final village

井頭上村

Boxing clever: communal mail delivery

The West Rail Station is straight ahead. Buses 67M, 67X and itinerant minibuses all follow the Tuen Mun Road towards Kowloon. Or you can walk to the Tuen Mun Centre to pick up the 961 bus, which runs directly to Hong Kong Island via the Western Harbour Tunnel. To get there, cross Castle Peak Road at the traffic lights on your left, and head up the covered stairway. On reaching the overhead walkway the bus depot is sign-posted. Bear left through two shopping malls and descend again by escalator to street level. At this point it's best to ask for further directions. Here the locals are very friendly. I came across a volunteer guide who was so taken by my depleted appearance, in boots, backpack and wilted hat looking so out of place in an air-conditioned shopping mall, that he literally took me by the hand and guided me to the 961 bus stop.

Trailwalker Route Change

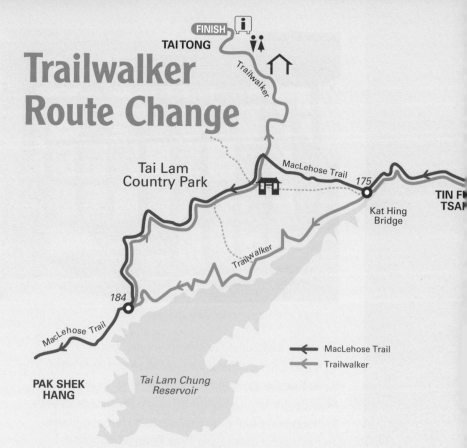

FINISH

TAI TONG

Trailwalker

Tai Lam
Country Park

MacLehose Trail

175

TIN F
TSA

Kat Hing
Bridge

Trailwalker

184

MacLehose Trail

⬅ MacLehose Trail

⬅ Trailwalker

PAK SHEK
HANG

Tai Lam Chung
Reservoir

Unique among city hikes and walks worldwide, the Oxfam Trailwalker is held annually on the MacLehose Trail, an adventurous and arduous 100 km hike across beautiful and natural scenery over the mountain ranges of the New Territories. Formerly a military drill for Gurkha soldiers, the annual event is supported with the sponsorship of many community organisations. Since 1986, more than 42,000 hikers have raised over HK$160 million in support of Oxfam's poverty alleviation and emergency relief projects. Although the Trailwalker hike follows the course of the MacLehose Trail for roughly 95% of the way, route changes have recently been introduced offering an alternative ending.

Passing through the valley of Tin Fu Tsai, near *M175*, the MacLehose parts company from the Trailwalker as it is redirected uphill on the tarmac service road away from its previous course along the reservoir. At this point however, the Trailwalker continues as before – along the shoreline of the Tai Lam Chung Reservoir. Just past *TW184*, the path mounts a set of steps and once again joins a service road. Turn right and follow the newly created route signs. Here Trailwalkers hike opposite to the MacLehose hikers to reach the finishing post, which is clearly signposted.

The beginning is easy – continuing is the hard part

Flood Warning

You may have seen the signs, or you may have not. Beware of flash floods, they warn, but the signs are often small, obscured by foliage, or covered with dark green mould. If you look, you'll find them placed either side of seemingly dry gullies on hillsides and in forests. Despite their subtlety, their warning is serious: flash floods are known to take lives.

Since the 1950s, when 28 people were washed into Tolo Harbour by a flash flood at Tai Po Kau, the government has built extensive catchment systems to divert hill water into reservoirs. But during the rainy season, things can get quickly out of hand, and a trickle can become a torrent with little warning. Take care when crossing watercourses.

An overland trip along the Silk Road took **Pete Spurrier** from London to China in 1993, and he has lived in Hong Kong since then, exploring the city's backstreets and hiking its hills. When not bribing sampan ladies to transport him to distant islands, he spends his time deciphering the secret language of minibus drivers. Pete's guided walks have appeared in the *South China Morning Post*, in local magazines, and in *The Leisurely and Heritage Hiker's Guide*, also published by FormAsia Books.

Addendum:

Since the first edition of this guidebook was published, we've been delighted to receive questions and feedback from hiking readers. Much of this has helped us update the guide each time. One query stands out: What to do if you're an overseas visitor to Hong Kong, with perhaps a day or two spare to tread the trails after a business trip or family visit? You are unlikely to know where the free country park campsites are located, or where to buy walking gear, stove gas and other outdoors necessities. With this in mind, we list the following websites as sources of useful information.

Outdoor Specialists:
http://www.chamonix.com.hk/shop.html
http://www.alink.com.hk/
http://www.protrek.com.hk/index.php?lang=en

HKSAR recommended campsites:
http://www.afcd.gov.hk/english/country/cou_vis/cou_vis_cam/cou_vis_cam_cam/cou_vis_cam_cam.html

The Serious Hiker's Guide to Hong Kong

Published by:
FormAsia Books Limited
706 Yu Yuet Lai Building
45 Wyndham Street
Central, Hong Kong
www.formasiabooks.com

Ninth Edition Published 2014
ISBN 978-988-98269-2-5

Text and photographs
©FormAsia Books Limited

Written by Pete Spurrier
Photography by Kwan Kwong Chung/
Sathish Gobinath

Produced by Format Limited, Hong Kong
Design: Alice Yim/Maggie Wan
Digital production: Nelson Pun/
Dickson Chou/Fred Yuen
Maps: Dickson Chou/Edwin Chiu/
Sunny Chan
Production supervision: Jenny Choi

Printed in Hong Kong by
Treasure Printing Company Limited
Images scanned by
Sky Art Graphic Company Limited, Hong Kong